small summer gardens

small summer gardens

35 bright and beautiful projects to bring color and scent to your garden

emma hardy

CICO BOOKS
LONDON NEW YORK

This paperback edition published in 2022 by CICO Books
An imprint of Ryland Peters & Small Ltd

20–21 Jockey's Fields   341 E 116th St
London WC1R 4BW   New York, NY 10029

www.rylandpeters.com

10 9 8 7 6 5 4 3 2 1

First published in 2018

A CIP catalog record for this book is available from the Library of Congress and the British Library.

ISBN: 978-1-80065-216-3

Printed in China

Editor: Caroline West
Designer: Luana Gobbo
Photographer: Debbie Patterson
Stylist: Emma Hardy

In-house editor: Anna Galkina
Art director: Sally Powell
Production controller: Mai-Ling Collyer
Publishing manager: Penny Craig
Publisher: Cindy Richards

MIX
Paper from responsible sources
FSC® C106563
www.fsc.org

contents

introduction

The garden comes into its own in summer, with such a wide selection of foliage and flowering plants looking their best. The summer months provide the perfect opportunity to spend time outside, enjoying the long daylight hours and, hopefully, some good weather. This is also the perfect season for creating beautiful planters to brighten up your garden and home. Whether you have a large garden with sufficient room for entertaining or just a modest window ledge or doorstep, there are planting ideas to suit every type of outdoor space.

Visit any garden center during the summer and the huge selection of plants on offer can seem overwhelming, so the idea behind this book is to provide ideas and inspiration so you can create your own special displays. I love using old containers, which can be bought in second-hand stores and online, for my planting displays. These usually have the added advantage of being relatively inexpensive, but there is also a wonderful array of new pots, window boxes, and planters available, all of which can look beautiful, too.

The book features 35 projects for container gardens, from tiny terracotta pots packed with pretty flowers to large tubs that create the effect of an herbaceous border. There are ideas for both indoor and outdoor gardening, as well as sections on edible gardening and foliage displays. A useful section on containers for special occasions offers more short-term planting ideas. Each project provides a list of plants to use (you'll usually need only one of each plant, unless stated otherwise). You can either follow these plant lists like a recipe, or use them purely for inspiration for successful color schemes and planting combinations. You may find that some of the suggested plants are not well suited to your area or are difficult to get hold of (although I have tried to use plants that are relatively easy to cultivate). However, using alternatives in similar colors and sizes will work just as well.

There is a handy section on materials and techniques, which gives advice on how to get started. Hopefully, this will help you not only to create beautiful planters, but also to keep them looking good for longer. Before you start planting, it is a good idea to put together a basic tool kit—if you buy the best tools you can afford and look after them well, they should last you for many years to come.

There are so many beautiful plants available in the summer that creating fabulous planters is a pure joy, and one that can be enjoyed for many months. I have really relished putting together the planting schemes for this book, and I hope you will gain equal pleasure from them, whether you stick closely to the projects or use them as a starting point for your own ideas.

Have fun creating fabulous planted containers and enjoy your summer garden!

MATERIALS and TECHNIQUES

I always think gardening is more enjoyable when you just "have a go," rather than getting bogged down with lots of advice, which can be a little overwhelming—especially for beginners. Having said that, it can be useful to learn a few basics before you begin to avoid making expensive mistakes. With this in mind, I have put together some tips and gentle advice to help you on your way.

CHOOSING CONTAINERS

There are pots, planters, troughs, window boxes, and hanging baskets available in a range of sizes, shapes, materials, and colors from garden centers and online. When deciding on a container, consider materials and colors that will offset your chosen plants well, or stick to classic terracotta, which looks good planted with just about anything. I love the look of old enamel and galvanized metal containers, which you can often pick up cheaply from second-hand stores and markets. Look out for old cans and boxes, as these make lovely containers, and also old pails (buckets) and tubs, which might not look very promising at first, but can be transformed by pretty planting.

PREPARING CONTAINERS

Before planting up a container, there are a few simple steps you can take to get your new plants off to a good start.

Making drainage holes

An important point to bear in mind when choosing containers is that they should ideally have drainage holes in the bottom, as most plants do not like sitting in very wet soil. However, you can easily make holes in containers made from materials like metal or wood with a hammer and large, heavy-duty nail. Simply turn the container upside down and hit the nail hard with the hammer to make several holes randomly around the base. You can also use an electric drill to make the holes.

If you can't make holes in a container, perhaps because it is made from stone, china, or terracotta, then use it for indoor planting or keep it in a covered area outside so that you can ensure the potting mix does not become waterlogged.

Use a hammer and sturdy nail to make a few drainage holes in the base of suitable containers.

Cleaning containers

To help prevent pests and diseases damaging your plants, clean containers before planting. Scrub them with warm, soapy water, rinse thoroughly, and let dry.

Using drainage crocks

Crocks are bits of old, broken terracotta pot, china, or old tiles that can be placed over the drainage holes at the bottom of a container to prevent them becoming blocked with potting mix, thus improving drainage. To make crocks, put the broken pots, etc. in a plastic bag (to prevent bits from hitting you), or wear protective goggles, and smash them up with a hammer. Aim for pieces that are roughly 1¼–1½in (3–4cm) square. Add a few handfuls of drainage crocks to the bottom of the container before planting. Set aside a supply of crocks for future displays.

BUYING AND PREPARING PLANTS

Always start with healthy plants, buying them from reputable suppliers and, if you can, take the plant out of its pot and inspect it before buying. Check the plant is not pot-bound, is disease-free, and has healthy-looking roots, leaves, and flowers. Also choose plants suitable for the size of the container and ensure there is ample space for the roots. For small planters, look for alpine and dwarf varieties, which will live happily in more cramped conditions.

Soaking plant roots

Give your container plants the best start by soaking their rootballs in water before planting. Immerse the rootballs in a pail (bucket) of water for 10–20 minutes, or until they are soaked through. Larger plants will need 20 minutes, but 10 minutes should suffice for plants with small rootballs.

Loosening plant roots

If you find that the roots of a plant look pot-bound when you remove the plant from its plastic pot for planting, it has probably been growing in the same pot for too long. Gently loosen the roots to encourage them to spread out and grow in the new pot.

Gently loosen the roots of pot-bound plants, being careful not to damage them as you do so. This encourages the roots to spread out in the new container.

POTTING MIXES

You'll find a wide selection of potting mixes at garden centers and online. Learning a little about the different types of potting mix will help you to select the correct one for each planting display. There are two main types: soil-based potting mix and soil-less potting mix (which contains peat or a peat substitute).

Soil-based potting mix

Soil-based potting mix is a good, all-purpose mix that is suitable for most container displays. It provides plants with decent nutrition for the weeks immediately after planting and also retains moisture. In addition, its free-draining qualities encourage roots to grow. Soil-based potting mix is ideal for a range of applications, including:

- **Seeds and cuttings:** Potting mixes for growing seeds and cuttings must be sterile, lightweight, and nutrient-poor (as too many nutrients can scorch newly germinated seedlings). The seedlings will need potting on to bigger pots as they grow.

- **Annuals and perennials:** These plants require a richer potting mix than seeds and cuttings, with a higher nutrient content to encourage root and foliage growth. Also available is bulb potting mix, a specialist mix that contains added grit or sand to provide a free-draining growing medium suitable for growing bulbs.

- **Permanent plantings:** Container plants must obtain all their nutrients from the potting mix. For this reason, plants such as the hydrangea in the *Rusty Planter with Daisies and Snapdragons* (see pages 36–39) and the *Potted Kumquat* (see pages 130–33), which are grown permanently in a container, need a potting mix that is rich in nutrients, with slow-release fertilizers, and also free-draining.

Soil-less potting mix

You can also buy soil-less potting mix, but this is better suited to short-term plantings because it is much lighter and tends to dry out very quickly. You will need to feed plants grown in this type of potting mix regularly to maintain nutrient levels, which tend to be low. It is, however, often cheaper than soil-based potting mixes and can be useful in small containers. Always try to avoid potting mixes that contain peat, as their production is very damaging to the environment.

Specialist potting mixes

For certain types of plant, a specific or "specialist" potting mix is necessary if they are to thrive. Plants that require a specialist potting mix include cacti and succulents, which need extra grit for drainage. If you can't get hold of any cactus and succulent potting mix, a general-purpose potting mix with added horticultural grit or gravel will work fine. Ericaceous plants, such as heathers, blueberries, and some ferns, are lime-hating and need an ericaceous potting mix with a pH lower than 7. This is often available in smaller bags, making it more economical to buy.

Incorporating additives

Container displays can benefit from various additives being mixed into the potting mix before the plants go in. While not essential, these additives can be very useful. Horticultural sand or grit, for example, can be used to improve drainage. This is especially important when growing cacti, succulents, and alpines, all of which prefer a free-draining growing medium. Only use sand or fine gravel for seedlings or very small plants, to avoid damaging their roots.

Vermiculite, which is an expanded mineral, and perlite, a naturally occurring volcanic glass, both improve drainage and help aerate the potting mix. They should be available from garden centers or online, and can often be bought in small quantities, which is useful for small-scale gardening.

Mulches and decorative trims

Mulches are materials that are spread over the surface of the potting mix to help preserve moisture, protect plant roots from extreme temperatures, or purely as a decorative finish.

Gravel, which is available in a wide variety of colors and sizes, adds a lovely finishing touch to container plantings and can also help to keep leaves off damp potting mix, so preventing them from rotting and causing disease. Gravel is traditionally used around cacti and succulents.

Slate, pebbles, pieces of broken glass, and shells are also readily available and can look very pretty when used as a mulch. Wood chippings and bark can also be used as mulches, although they are more useful for large-scale plantings. Sheet and cushion moss, available from florists and garden centers, both provide a natural-looking cover for the surface of the potting mix and can finish off a planting scheme beautifully.

CARING FOR PLANTS

Looking after container plants well is important and will help to keep them looking good for longer. Follow these simple tips and your plants will bloom throughout the summer season.

Watering

Container gardens are particularly prone to drying out, especially in warm weather, so it is essential to check the potting mix regularly and water as required. Try to water in the evening rather than the morning, to reduce the rate of evaporation. Generally, plants need more water during their growing season, over the summer, and much less in winter.

Most plants prefer moist rather than soaking-wet potting mix, but do not like to dry out completely. Check your containers daily, particularly in warm weather. A good way to check moisture levels in a container is to stick your finger in the potting mix, as the surface can sometimes look wet but be dry underneath. If the potting mix feels dry, then you need to water the container.

You can also add moisture-retaining granules to the potting mix when planting up your containers. Although not essential, these can be useful for small containers, hanging baskets, and indoor displays that are prone to drying out quickly.

If your plants start to look unhappy, try changing the watering regime or moving them to a different spot. In very hot weather, for example, you may need to water your containers twice daily. Also, if the sun is particularly strong, it might be worth moving the containers into the shade to provide some protection.

If a container feels very dry, plunge the whole thing into a large tub of water and let it soak thoroughly. Leave the plant soaking for at least half an hour, then remove and let drain.

Feeding

Most general-purpose potting mixes provide plants with enough nutrients for six to eight weeks following planting. After this time, container-grown plants benefit from additional feeding on a regular basis, in the form of either liquid feeds or slow-release fertilizer granules. Regular feeding is especially important for flowering and fruiting plants.

* **Liquid feeds:** These are available for either general use or specific types of plant, such as tomatoes,

Top: *Plants grown in containers or confined spaces, such as this raised bed, can dry out quickly. Remember to water plants regularly, preferably in the evening.*

Above: *Regularly feeding container-grown plants with a liquid feed, diluted according to the manufacturer's instructions, will result in healthier plants.*

roses, or strawberries. Following the manufacturer's instructions, the feed can be diluted and added either weekly or fortnightly throughout the growing season. Liquid feeds are a good buy and work well for most outdoor containers.

* **Slow-release fertilizer granules:** You can add these to the potting mix before planting or roughly fork them into the top of the potting mix in established containers. This type of fertilizer reduces the need for regular liquid feeds.

* **Foliar feeds:** These are great options for giving your container plants a quick boost. They are diluted liquid fertilizers that are sprayed directly onto plants to perk them up quickly, but are not a substitute for feeding the potting mix. Don't spray the plant in direct sunlight, because the leaves may scorch as the solution dries.

Deadheading

To promote new growth, dead flower heads and leaves must be removed from container-grown plants. This can increase flowering by encouraging the plants to put their energy into producing new flowers rather than setting seed, while also keeping them looking neat and tidy. Remove the dead flower heads and leaves by hand, or use a pair of scissors or hand pruners (secateurs) if the stems are harder or woodier. This approach also reduces the risk of pest and disease infestation.

Staking

Some plants, such as dahlias, delphiniums, achilleas, and pepper plants, can grow quite tall. Staking provides additional support and stops the stems bending over and looking untidy. Simply use garden twine, string, or colorful raffia to tie the stems to garden canes or twiggy stems pushed into the potting mix.

Top: *Removing spent blooms from plants—a technique known as deadheading—can promote further flushes of flowers.*

Above: *Support taller plants by tying their stems to garden canes or twiggy stems pushed into the potting mix. Here, pretty raffia is being used to tie in some pepper plants.*

DEALING WITH PESTS AND DISEASES

If unchecked, pests and diseases can quickly decimate your plants and garden. Vigilance, as well as acting quickly upon the first signs of an infestation, is good practice for keeping your plants and containers healthy and looking good for as long as possible. Here are some useful tips to help keep your displays in tip-top condition:

* Always clean containers thoroughly before planting.

* Buy strong-looking plants with healthy rootballs and no obvious signs of disease. You can check for possible problems by removing the plant from its pot and inspecting it before purchasing.

* Make sure you use a good-quality potting mix that is correct for the plants you're growing, and keep the container in a suitable spot, both to encourage healthy growth and to reduce the risk of disease.

* Feeding regularly results in healthier plants, making them less likely to succumb to problems.

* Check your plants regularly for signs of pest and disease infestation.

* If possible, use organic products to help combat any pests and diseases. Other commercially available treatments risk harming welcome wildlife, which can help to reduce pest infestations naturally.

Aphids (blackfly and greenfly) must be removed at first sight. They suck the sap from plants, resulting in a lack of vigor and, ultimately, distorted growth. A light infestation can be removed with your fingers, although commercial treatments are available for heavier infestations. If you are unsure about using chemicals in the garden, spraying with a dilute solution of water and dishwashing detergent can work well too.

Botrytis (gray mold) is a fungal infection that occurs if plants are damp and have insufficient ventilation. It is a common problem, characterized by a quick-spreading, gray, dusty mold on the stems and leaves of plants. To remedy this, use an organic fungicide and improve ventilation. Be careful not to confuse gray mold with dehydration, a telltale sign of which is a similar whitish bloom on the foliage; this should be remedied with additional watering and feeding.

CONTAINER GARDENING KIT

You don't need lots of expensive equipment to enjoy container gardening. Below is a list of recommended items that will get you off to a flying start.

Garden canes or twiggy branches
(for staking plants)

Garden trowel

Gardening gloves

Hammer and large, heavy-duty nail
(for making drainage holes in containers)

Hand fork

Hand pruners (secateurs)

Plant labels and waterproof pen

Scissors

String and/or garden twine

Watering can, with a fine rose attachment

Water spray bottle

CHAPTER 1

BRIGHT FLORALS AND SCENTS

green enamel CONTAINER

This vintage enamel pail (bucket) is packed full of pretty flowering plants in delicate shades of purple, mauve, and pink, creating a charming summer planter. Many of the flowers have a beautiful fragrance, so make the most of these delicious scents by positioning the planter near a seating area or in a part of the garden that you visit often during the day.

YOU WILL NEED

Metal pail (bucket)

Hammer and heavy-duty nail

Drainage crocks

Potting mix

plants:

Calibrachoa Minifamous Series Double Pink (mini petunia)

Nemesia Nuvo Series

Phlox subulata 'Alexander's Surprise', *P. subulata* 'Candy Stripe', and *P. subulata* 'Kimono' (moss phlox)

Syringa pubescens subsp. *patula* (Manchurian lilac)

1 Soak the rootballs of all the plants in water for about 20 minutes, or until they are wet through. Use the hammer and nail to make drainage holes in the bottom of the pail (bucket)—for advice on how to do this, see page 8. Cover the holes with a few crocks to improve drainage. Half-fill the container with potting mix and level off the surface.

2 Remove the lilac from its plastic pot and plant it at the back of the pail. Add or remove potting mix, as required, so the top of the plant's rootball is sitting just below the rim of the pail.

3 Position the larger plants around the lilac, planting them in the same way as before and ensuring the tops of all the rootballs are level.

4 Plant the smaller plants around the front of the pail, removing them from their plastic pots and letting them trail decoratively over the edge. Add handfuls of potting mix to fill any gaps between the plants. Water the pail and let drain.

AFTERCARE

Check the potting mix in the container regularly and ensure it is kept moist, as the plants won't like to dry out. Water in some general-purpose fertilizer every couple of weeks to prolong the flowering period.

rusty trunk WITH FOXGLOVES

This rusty, old, metal trunk looks stunning planted with pink and white foxgloves and cow parsley. Using delicate, feathery plants such as cow parsley and geum softens the strong, bold look of the foxgloves and creates a delightfully elegant planter.

YOU WILL NEED

Large metal trunk or tub

Hammer and heavy-duty nail (optional)

Drainage crocks

Potting mix

plants:

Anthriscus sylvestris 'Ravenswing' (cow parsley)

Cytisus × *praecox* 'Allgold' (broom)

Digitalis purpurea 'Dalmatian Rose' and *D. purpurea* 'Dalmatian White' (foxglove)

Geum rivale 'Album' (water avens)

1 Soak the rootballs of all the plants in water for about 20 minutes, or until they are wet through. If necessary, use the hammer and nail to make drainage holes in the bottom of the container (see page 8). Cover the holes with drainage crocks so they will not become blocked with potting mix, which will impede drainage.

2 Half-fill the container with potting mix, spreading it out evenly and leveling the surface.

3 Take the foxgloves from their plastic pots and arrange them in the container. Add or remove potting mix, as necessary, so the top of each plant's rootball is sitting just under the rim.

4 Remove the cow parsley from its plastic pot and plant it in the center of the container, adjusting the depth of the potting mix, as you did before.

5 Plant the broom in the same way, positioning it at the front of the container.

6 Finally, take the geum from its plastic pot and squeeze it between the other plants.

7 Add more potting mix to fill any gaps between the plants and level off the surface, making sure there are no air pockets. Water the container and let drain.

BEAUTY in a black bowl

The stunning colors of these plants are offset beautifully by the dark finish of the bowl. Choosing a striking black or dark gray planter makes a great style statement, as it contrasts starkly with the pretty pale orange and peach colors of the flowers. The result is a stunning planter that is positively bursting with blooms.

YOU WILL NEED

Large metal bowl

Hammer and heavy-duty nail

Drainage crocks

Potting mix

plants:

1 *Digitalis* 'Goldcrest' (foxglove hybrid)

2 *Geum* 'Mai Tai' (avens)

1 *Sanguisorba menziesii* (Menzies' burnet)

1 *Verbascum* 'Southern Charm' (mullein)

1 Soak the rootballs of all the plants in water for about 10 minutes, or until they are wet through. Use the hammer and nail to make drainage holes in the bottom of the bowl (see page 8). Cover the holes with drainage crocks, to prevent them becoming clogged with potting mix.

2 Add some potting mix to the bowl, spreading it over the crocks.

AFTERCARE

Keep the potting mix moist and remember to deadhead regularly. This will encourage further flushes of flowers.

3 Take the digitalis from its plastic pot, loosen the roots slightly around the rootball, and plant it in the middle of the bowl.

4 Remove the geums from their plastic pots and plant one on each side of the digitalis. Firm the potting mix down well to hold the plants in place.

5 Take the sanguisorba from its plastic pot and plant it next to the digitalis and geums.

6 Finally, remove the small verbascum from its plastic pot and plant it toward the edge of the bowl, at the front.

7 Add a few handfuls of potting mix to fill any gaps between the plants. Press the surface down firmly to keep the plants in place. Water the bowl and let drain.

metal tub WITH MINI ROSES

I love rose gardens, and this pretty, low-growing rose, which is repeat-flowering, creates a beautiful miniature rose garden in a galvanized metal tub. The lychnis, with its little pom-pom flowers, softens the look, while the argyranthemum and tiarella add further floral interest.

YOU WILL NEED

Large galvanized metal tub

Hammer and heavy-duty nail (optional)

Drainage crocks

Potting mix

plants:

2–3 *Argyranthemum* 'Aramis Fire' (marguerite)

1 *Lychnis flos-cuculi* 'Petite Jenny' (ragged robin)

1 *Rosa* 'Morsdag' (rose)

1 *Tiarella* 'Spring Symphony' (foam flower)

1 Soak the rootballs of all the plants in water for about 20 minutes, or until they are wet through. If necessary, use the hammer and nail to make drainage holes in the bottom of the tub (see page 8). Cover the holes with drainage crocks to prevent them becoming blocked with potting mix.

2 Half-fill the tub with potting mix and level off the surface.

AFTERCARE

It is important to keep the potting mix moist and to deadhead the flowers regularly if you want to keep them flowering throughout the summer. Use a general-purpose fertilizer every couple of weeks over spring and summer, following the manufacturer's instructions.

3 Remove the rose from its plastic pot and plant it toward one side of the tub.

4 Take the lychnis from its plastic pot next and plant it in the tub, adding or removing potting mix, as required, so the plant is sitting at the same level as the rose.

5 Remove the tiarella from its plastic pot and plant it in the same way, but this time positioning it at the edge of the tub.

6 Plant the argyranthemums, removing them from their plastic pots and tucking them into the spaces between the other plants.

7 Add more potting mix to fill any gaps between the plants. Press down the surface of the potting mix to hold the plants in place. Water the tub and let drain.

fragrant SWEET PEA container

I have never managed to grow sweet peas very successfully in my flower borders, so thought I would try growing them in a container. Being able to give them a rich potting mix, with plenty of room for their roots, and feeding them regularly has produced a much more abundant display, and I shall definitely grow them like this again. Adding a few twiggy supports creates the perfect framework for the sweet peas to scramble up. Here, I have shown how to grow sweet peas from seed, but you can skip the seed-sowing stage, if you wish, and buy in garden-ready plug plants from a garden center or nursery, or online, instead.

YOU WILL NEED

Small plastic pots (optional)

Seed potting mix (optional)

Watering can, with fine rose attachment

Clear plastic bag or plastic wrap/clingfilm (optional)

Large planter or tub

Hammer and heavy-duty nail (optional)

Drainage crocks

Potting mix

Twiggy branches and garden twine, to support the growing sweet peas

plants:

A selection of *Lathyrus odoratus* (sweet pea) seeds or plug plants, such as 'Barry Dare', 'Black Knight', 'Lord Nelson', and 'Matucana'

Nemesia Nuvo Series 'Nuvo Rose' (optional)

2 To make your sweet pea plants nice and bushy, nip off the top growth of each seedling, down to two leaves, when they are a few inches tall. This will encourage the plants to grow out rather than just upward.

3 Prepare your chosen container. If necessary, use the hammer and nail to make drainage holes in the bottom of the container (see page 8). Cover the holes with drainage crocks to prevent them getting blocked with potting mix. Fill the container with potting mix.

1 If you have bought sweet pea plants, skip Steps 1 and 2, and begin with Step 3. If you are growing the sweet peas from seed, the best time to sow them is any time between mid-fall (autumn) and early spring. Fill the small plastic pots with seed potting mix and level off the surface. Plant three sweet pea seeds in each pot and cover with about ½in (1cm) of the potting mix. Water the pots, using a fine rose attachment on the watering can to avoid disturbing the seeds, then cover them with a clear plastic bag or piece of plastic wrap (clingfilm). This keeps in warmth and moisture. Leave the pots in a warm spot—a garden shed or cold frame is fine—until the seeds start to germinate. Check each day to see if your seeds have germinated. Once they have, remove the coverings and wait until the seedlings are a few inches tall before going on to the next step.

4 Push the end of a twiggy branch into the potting mix on one side of the container, so it is sitting nice and upright.

5 Continue to add more branches to the container, spacing them out evenly, as shown. I used six branches in this metal planter.

AFTERCARE

Use a general-purpose fertilizer weekly to encourage lots of sweet pea flowers. Pick the flowers every few days. This will not only give you deliciously fragrant flowers for the house, but also encourage new growth.

6 Remove the sweet pea seedlings from their plastic pots and plant them at the bases of the branches, planting them so the tops of their rootballs are level with the potting mix in the container.

7 Gently tie the seedlings to the branches using garden twine, being careful not to damage them. If you wish, plant nemesia around the edge of the container to provide further color. Water the container and keep it moist.

WOODEN tray with zinnias

This wooden-tray display is perfect for the summer garden, as it is so pretty and colorful. It looks all the better for being planted with an abundance of blooms and, because zinnias can often be bought quite cheaply in nurseries, it's a good idea to buy lots of them and really pack them in!

YOU WILL NEED

Large wooden tray

Black plastic sheeting (optional)

Staple gun and staples (optional)

Potting mix

plants:

A selection of zinnias, such as *Zinnia elegans* Magellan Mixed, *Z. marylandica* Zahara Fire, and *Z. marylandica* Zahara Red

1 Soak the rootballs of all the zinnias in water for about 10 minutes. You may want to protect the wooden tray, as I did here, by lining it with black plastic sheeting. Simply cut a piece of sheeting large enough to line the tray. Lay the sheeting in the tray, tuck it neatly into the corners, and use the staple gun around the top edge of the tray to fix it in place.

2 Half-fill the tray with potting mix and level off the surface.

3 Plant the first zinnia in the tray, removing it from its plastic pot and firming the potting mix around the roots slightly to keep the plant standing upright.

4 Continue planting the other zinnias in the tray in the same way, adding more potting mix to hold them in place and firmly pressing down the surface. Try to achieve a varied and interesting mix of colors throughout the display. Water the tray and let drain.

AFTERCARE

This wooden tray did not have any drainage holes. If that is the case with your tray, make sure you don't over-water the zinnias—just keep the potting mix moist. Also deadhead the flowers regularly to ensure further flushes of flowers.

RUSTY PLANTER with daisies and snapdragons

I love the combination of white flowers and a grass in this planter. The plants are set off beautifully by the lovely rust-colored pail (bucket). Keeping color schemes simple in this way and bringing in prairie-style grasses creates a charming planter that will look good for months on end.

YOU WILL NEED

Large metal pail (bucket)

Hammer and heavy-duty nail (optional)

Drainage crocks

Potting mix

plants:

1 *Anthemis* 'Tetworth'

3–4 *Antirrhinum majus* 'Twinny White' (snapdragon)

1 *Hydrangea paniculata* 'Kyushu'

1 *Stipa tenuissima* (Mexican feather grass)

1 Soak the rootballs of all the plants in water for about 20 minutes, or until they are wet through. If necessary, use the hammer and nail to make drainage holes in the bottom of the pail (bucket)—for advice on how to do this, see page 8. Cover the holes with a few drainage crocks to prevent them getting blocked with potting mix.

2 Add potting mix to the bottom of the pail until it is about half full, then level off the surface.

AFTERCARE

Deadhead the flowering plants regularly to promote further flowers and use a general-purpose fertilizer every few weeks, as the hydrangea will be quite greedy and use up the nutrients in the potting mix.

3 Take the hydrangea from its plastic pot first and plant it toward the back of the pail.

4 Remove the grass from its pot and plant it next to the hydrangea, adding or removing potting mix, as required, so the tops of the plants' rootballs are level. Plant the anthemis next to the first two plants in the same way.

5 If a plant is looking a little pot-bound when you remove it from its plastic pot—in this case, one of the antirrhinums—loosen the rootball gently with your fingers.

6 Plant the antirrhinums around the edge of the pail.

7 Fill any gaps between the plants with more potting mix, as necessary, and level off the surface, pressing it down slightly. Water the pail and let drain.

rustic orange tray with bright FLOWERS

This old painted tray came from a tabletop sale and looked rather uninspiring at first. Planting it with striking orange flowers, and softening the look with some delicately dotty gypsophila and androsace, really brings the tray to life and creates a stunning summer garden.

YOU WILL NEED

Large, deep metal tray

Hammer and heavy-duty nail

Drainage crocks

Potting mix

Sheet moss (available from garden centers and florists)

plants:

2 *Androsace septentrionalis* 'Stardust' (pygmyflower rock jasmine)

2 *Bidens ferulifolia* 'Blazing Glory'

2 *Dahlia* 'Bishop of Oxford'

2 *Erigeron karvinskianus* (Mexican fleabane)

1 *Geum coccineum* 'Koi'

1 *Gypsophila paniculata* (baby's breath)

2 *Helianthemum* 'Hartswood Ruby' (rock rose)

1 Soak the rootballs of all the plants in water for about 10 minutes, or until they are wet through. Use the hammer and nail to make drainage holes in the base of the tray (see page 8). Cover the holes with drainage crocks, so they do not become blocked with potting mix.

2 Add potting mix to the tray, filling it halfway and leveling off the surface.

3 Take the dahlias from their plastic pots first and loosen the potting mix around the rootballs slightly, being careful not to damage the roots. Plant the dahlias at opposite ends of the tray.

4 Remove the androsace and gypsophila from their plastic pots next and plant them in the same way. Repeat with the geum and rock rose, arranging them to create an attractive effect.

5 Tuck the erigeron plants around the sides of the tray, planting them so they will trail over the edge.

6 Add more potting mix around the roots of the plants to fill in any holes and level off the surface.

7 Use pieces of sheet moss to disguise the potting mix until the plants have grown large enough. Water the tray and let drain.

AFTERCARE

Keep the potting mix damp. This is one of those planting displays that will benefit from regular deadheading, to keep the blooms going for longer.

olive container with EUPHORBIA

Old olive pails (buckets) were once used during the olive harvest to pick and wash the olives. They make attractive and practical garden planters, having the advantage of ready-made drainage holes. They are also large enough to accommodate several plants. In this display, the lime-green of the euphorbia works beautifully with the deep reds and purples of the aquilegia and astrantia, with a few simple cream anemones positioned at the front of the container to finish the look.

1 Soak the rootballs of all the plants in water for about 20 minutes, or until they are wet through. Meanwhile, add a few drainage crocks to the base of the pail (bucket) and then line the base and sides with pieces of moss, to stop the potting mix from escaping through the holes. Add handfuls of potting mix as you go, to help keep the moss in place.

2 Add more potting mix, pressing it down firmly and ensuring there are no air pockets. Press the potting mix against the sides of the pail to keep the moss in place, but make sure you leave enough room for the plants.

YOU WILL NEED

Old olive-harvesting pail (bucket)

Drainage crocks

Sheet moss (available from garden centers and florists)

Potting mix

plants:

2 *Anemone magellanica* (windflower)

1 each of *Aquilegia* State Series 'Louisiana' and *A. vulgaris* var. *stellata* 'Nora Barlow' (columbine)

1 *Astrantia major* Gill Richardson Group (masterwort)

1 *Euphorbia* × *martini* 'Ascot Rainbow' (Martin's spurge)

3 Take the aquilegias from their plastic pots and plant them at the back of the pail.

4 Next, remove the euphorbia from its plastic pot and plant it in front of the aquilegias.

5 Decide on a suitable position for the astrantia and plant it in the pail next. Firm down all the plants, so they are sitting nice and upright.

6 Take the anemones from their plastic pots and plant them at the front of the pail, positioning them to fill any gaps between the other flowers. Add a few handfuls of potting mix around the plants and firm down the surface.

7 Give the planter a decorative top-dressing by adding more moss to the surface of the potting mix. Water the pail and let drain.

blue enamel bowl with PURPLE FLOWERS

This bowl was planted when the allium bulbs and other plants were in bloom, but with a bit of planning you could plant the bulbs in the fall (autumn) and add the other plants the following spring. The allium flowers will fade before the other plants, but they look beautiful at all stages and will continue to add structure and shape to the planter long after the flowers have gone over.

YOU WILL NEED

Large enamel bowl

Hammer and heavy-duty nail

Drainage crocks

Potting mix

Fine gravel

plants:

3–4 *Allium hollandicum* 'Purple Sensation' (Dutch garlic)

1 *Baptisia* Decadence Series 'Dutch Chocolate' (false indigo)

1 each of *Delphinium* 'Highlander Flamenco', *D.* 'Magic Fountains Blue/ White Bee', and *D.* 'Magic Fountains Lilac Rose' (larkspur)

2 *Hesperis matronalis* (dame's violet)

1 each of *Salvia* × *sylvestris* 'Rhapsody in Blue' and *S.* × *sylvestris* 'Viola Klose' (wood sage)

1 Soak the rootballs of all the plants in water for about 10 minutes, or until they are wet through. Use the hammer and nail to make drainage holes in the bottom of the bowl (see page 8). Cover the holes with drainage crocks, to prevent them becoming blocked with potting mix.

2 Half-fill the bowl with potting mix, leveling off the surface.

3 Remove the alliums from their plastic pots and plant them in the bowl. Press the potting mix firmly around the rootballs, adding a few more handfuls if necessary so that they stand upright.

4 Take one of the delphiniums from its plastic pot and plant it toward one side of the bowl in the same way, firming the potting mix around it.

5 Remove one of the salvias from its plastic pot and plant it on the other side of the bowl, again pressing down the potting mix firmly to keep the plant in place.

6 Repeat the process for the remaining plants, arranging them among the first plants to form a pleasing display. Again, as all the plants are tall, firm them in well so they stand upright.

7 Use a few trowel-fuls of potting mix to fill any gaps between the plants, press down firmly, and level off the surface. Water the bowl and let drain.

8 As a decorative finishing touch, sprinkle fine gravel around the plants to cover the surface of the potting mix completely. The gravel also serves a practical purpose in helping to retain valuable moisture.

AFTERCARE

The plants in this display are all sun-lovers, so position the finished bowl in a sunny spot. Ensure you keep the potting mix damp. Stake the plants with garden twine tied to garden canes or twiggy branches pushed into the potting mix. This will help keep them upright.

PRETTY PLANTED basket

The mixture of plants in this two-tone basket creates the effect of a wildflower meadow. The basket would look equally lovely as a window box or tabletop decoration. I used a plastic storage basket, lined with a large plastic bag to prevent the potting mix from showing through the sides, but any rectangular basket or box is ideal.

YOU WILL NEED

Scissors

Large, white plastic bag

Large, deep plastic storage basket

Drainage crocks

Potting mix

plants:

Bidens 'Moonlight' (tickseed)

Cosmos atrosanguineus Chocamocha (chocolate cosmos)

Erigeron karvinskianus (Mexican fleabane)

Knautia macedonica 'Thunder and Lightning' (Macedonian scabious)

Linaria aeruginea 'Neon Lights' (toadflax)

Scabiosa japonica var. *alpina* 'Ritz Rose' (pincushion flower)

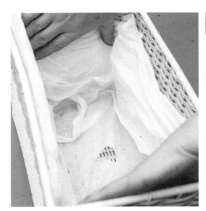

1 Soak the rootballs of all the plants in water for about 20 minutes, or until they are thoroughly wet. Cut a few small holes in the bottom of the plastic bag to allow for drainage. Open up the bag and place it in the basket to act as a liner and prevent the potting mix falling through the gaps in the sides. Push the bag into the corners of the basket, so that it fits snugly.

2 Put a few crocks in the bottom of the basket to help with drainage.

3 Half-fill the basket with potting mix and level off the surface.

4 Take the chocolate cosmos from its plastic pot and plant it toward the back of the basket. As you plant the cosmos, have a good sniff to take in its delicious chocolatey aroma.

5 Remove the erigeron from its plastic pot and plant it in front of the cosmos, allowing the flowers to drape slightly over the edge of the basket.

6 Take the knautia and scabiosa from their plastic pots and plant one at each end of the basket.

7 Plant the linaria at the front of the basket, ensuring that the tops of all the plants' rootballs are level.

8 Squeeze the bidens in last, adding or removing potting mix, as required, so that it fits snugly.

9 Fill any gaps between the plants with a few handfuls of potting mix and press the surface down slightly. Water the basket and let drain.

AFTERCARE

Deadhead the flowers regularly and feed the plants with a general-purpose fertilizer every week or so over the summer—this will help to keep them in tip-top condition.

enamel dish with DAHLIAS and ACHILLEAS

The stunning colors of these dahlias are offset beautifully by the simplicity of the cream enamel dish. Deadheading the dahlias regularly will encourage them to keep flowering. Pick a few gorgeous flowers when they are in full bloom, so you can enjoy them indoors too.

YOU WILL NEED

Large enamel dish

Hammer and heavy-duty nail

Drainage crocks

Potting mix

plants:

1 *Achillea* Galaxy Series 'Lachsschönheit' (yarrow)

2 each of *Dahlia* 'Mystic Fantasy' and *D.* 'Mystic Memories'

1 Soak the rootballs of all the plants in water for about 20 minutes, or until they are wet through. Use the hammer and nail to make drainage holes in the bottom of the dish (see page 8). Cover the drainage holes with crocks, so they do not become blocked with potting mix.

2 Add a few scoops of potting mix to the dish and level off the surface.

3 Take the dahlias from their plastic pots and plant them in the dish first, checking you are happy with their position as you go. A total of four dahlias were used in this dish. Try to position the tallest plant in the center and the shorter ones toward the edge.

4 Take the achillea from its plastic pot and plant it in the dish, making sure it is sitting firmly in place and will not topple over.

5 Add more potting mix to fill any spaces between the plants, firming it down well to hold them in place. Water the dish and let drain.

AFTERCARE

Keep the potting mix moist, but not too wet, and remember to deadhead the dahlias regularly, to keep them flowering and looking their best. Use a general-purpose fertilizer every few weeks in the summer, to keep the plants flourishing and healthy.

white pot with LAVENDER

This white pot works beautifully with the frosty color of the helichrysum and the delicate purple and blue of the lavender and catananche. There is also a shot of lime-green nicotiana through the planting to add a brighter punch of color. Position this pot by a frequently used door or path so you can enjoy the relaxing fragrance of the lavender, as well as the beauty of the display.

1 Soak the rootballs of all the plants in water for about 20 minutes, or until they are wet through. Cover the hole(s) in the pot with a few drainage crocks to stop them becoming blocked with potting mix.

2 Half-fill the pot with potting mix and spread it out evenly.

YOU WILL NEED
White pot
Drainage crocks
Potting mix

plants:
1 *Catananche caerulea* 'Amor Blue' (cupid's dart)

1 *Helichrysum petiolare* 'Goring Silver' (licorice plant)

1 *Lavandula angustifolia* 'Essence Purple' (English lavender)

4–6 *Nicotiana × sanderae* Cuba Series 'Cuba Deep Lime' (tobacco plant)

AFTERCARE

Keep the potting mix moist but not too wet, as the lavender—a plant that prefers full sun and well-drained soil—will not be happy with very wet roots. Deadhead the catananche and the nicotiana regularly to prolong their flowering period.

3 Take the catananche from its plastic pot first, as it is the largest plant, and plant it in the pot. Position the plant to one side of the pot, to add height to the arrangement at the back.

4 Plant the lavender in the same way, placing it next to the catananche and making sure the rootballs of both plants are level.

5 Remove the helichrysum from its plastic pot and plant it at the front of the pot, adding a little more potting mix if it is sitting too low and letting the stems trail slightly over the edge.

6 Lastly, remove the nicotianas from their plastic pots, plant a couple next to the helichrysum at the front of the pot, and dot the remainder throughout the display to create a pleasing arrangement. Add a few handfuls of potting mix to fill any gaps between the plants, pressing down the surface slightly. Water the pot and let drain.

COUNTRY GARDEN in metal tubs

YOU WILL NEED

Selection of galvanized metal tubs

Hammer and heavy-duty nail (optional)

Drainage crocks

Potting mix

plants:

A selection of pretty flowering plants, such as:

Allium cernuum (lady's leek)

1 each of *Delphinium* 'Magic Fountains Cherry Blossom/White Bee', *D.* Magic Fountains Lavender/White Bee', and *D.* 'Magic Fountains Lilac Pink'

Gypsophila paniculata (baby's breath)

Lavatera × clementii 'Bredon Springs' (tree mallow)

Salvia leucantha (Mexican bush sage)

Scabiosa caucasica 'Perfecta Blue' (Caucasian scabious)

Verbena bonariensis (Argentinian vervain)

Don't let a lack of space prevent you from creating a beautiful country garden. Simply gather together a few galvanized metal tubs and a selection of pretty flowering plants to create your own tiny country version. The taller plants may need staking to prevent the blooms from toppling over, so have a few garden canes or twiggy branches and garden twine at hand and tie them in place before the plants look as if they need it.

1 Soak the rootballs of all the plants in water for about 20 minutes, or until they are wet through. Make sure the tubs have drainage holes. If necessary, use the hammer and nail to make drainage holes in the bottom of the tubs (see page 8). Cover the drainage holes with crocks, so they do not become blocked with potting mix.

AFTERCARE

Keep the potting mix in the tubs moist at all times. Stake the plants with garden twine tied to garden canes or twiggy branches, especially if the tubs are in a windy spot. This will stop the stems bending and help keep them upright.

2 I planted the larger tub with handles first. Half-fill the tub with potting mix and spread it out evenly. Take the tallest plant from its plastic pot—in this case, the gypsophila—and plant it at the back of the tub. Firm down the potting mix to keep the plant in place and prevent it toppling over.

3 Remove the verbena from its plastic pot and plant it next to the first plant. Tease out the roots slightly, if the plant is looking pot-bound. Again, make sure the plant is sitting firmly in place, adding a little more potting mix, if necessary.

4 Take the delphiniums from their plastic pots and plant them in the middle of the tub.

5 Plant the salvia in the tub next, removing it from its plastic pot, tucking it in at the front, and pressing down the potting mix firmly to hold the plant in place.

6 Lastly, remove the allium from its plastic pot and plant it toward the front of the tub. Add more potting mix, as required, and press everything down firmly, so all the plants are sitting upright. Plant the other tubs with more country-garden plants. Here, I used a blue scabious and magenta lavatera. Water the tubs and let drain.

CHAPTER 2

LUSH FOLIAGE

SUCCULENTS in pretty pastel pots

Succulents are easy to look after and require little attention, so they make the perfect plants for novice gardeners. There are so many lovely shapes and sizes to choose from that you will probably have quite a collection in no time at all. A pretty way to display succulents is in colorful cups and pots, either grouped together on shelves or clustered on a tabletop.

1 Put some coarse gravel in the bottom of each pot to help break up the potting mix a little.

2 Add a small amount of potting mix to the bottom of the pots. Take the first plant from its plastic pot and loosen the rootball a little.

3 Place the plant in one of the pots and press down quite firmly to anchor it in place.

4 Add more potting mix to the pot if necessary to fill any gaps and level off the surface. Ensure the potting mix is sitting just under the rim of the pot so there will be room for a gravel top-dressing. Plant the other pots in the same way.

5 Add a good handful of fine gravel to cover the surface of the potting mix in each pot. This helps to conserve water and adds a nice finishing touch as well. Water the pots sparingly, leaving the potting mix to almost dry out before watering again.

GRASSES in metal containers

Summer gardening usually brings to mind borders and containers spilling over with flowering plants, but these grasses bring an understated charm to the summer garden. They will thrive in a sunny spot and, when grouped together, give a sophisticated look to any outside space.

YOU WILL NEED

Selection of metal containers in different shapes and sizes

Hammer and heavy-duty nail (optional)

Drainage crocks

Potting mix

Gravel, for top-dressing

plants:

Back left container: *Carex buchananii* (leatherleaf sedge) and *Pennisetum* × *advena* 'Rubrum' (fountain grass)

Back right container: *Carex testacea* (orange New Zealand sedge)

Front container: *Carex elata* 'Aurea' (Bowles' golden sedge), *C. oshimensis* 'Evergold' (Japanese sedge), and *Stipa tenuissima* (Mexican feather grass)

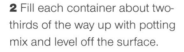

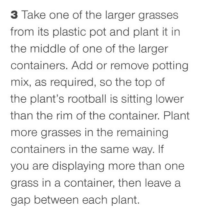

1 Soak the rootballs of all the grasses in water for about 20 minutes, or until they are wet through. If you are using an old food can or galvanized dish, or any of your containers don't already have drainage holes, you will need to make some in the base. Use the hammer and nail to make holes randomly all over the base of each container, as required (see page 8). Turn the containers the right way up and cover the holes with a few crocks to help improve drainage.

2 Fill each container about two-thirds of the way up with potting mix and level off the surface.

3 Take one of the larger grasses from its plastic pot and plant it in the middle of one of the larger containers. Add or remove potting mix, as required, so the top of the plant's rootball is sitting lower than the rim of the container. Plant more grasses in the remaining containers in the same way. If you are displaying more than one grass in a container, then leave a gap between each plant.

4 Add more potting mix to fill in any gaps remaining at the tops of the containers, press down, and level off the surface.

5 Put a few handfuls of gravel around the grasses and spread it out evenly to cover the potting mix. This adds a decorative touch and also helps to preserve water in the containers. Place the containers in a warm, sunny spot. Water and let drain.

INDOOR PLANTS in baskets

Houseplants have experienced something of a resurgence in recent years, and rightly so. As well as bringing nature into your home, they also help purify the air of chemicals from furniture, cleaning products, and decorating materials. Every household should have them. Houseplants are relatively easy to look after, provided they are not over-watered, and, once you have found a sheltered spot out of direct sunlight, they should thrive, looking beautiful and providing a valuable service.

1 You will need to display the plants in a light, draft-free place. Decide on a suitable spot and use the bradawl to make holes in the ceiling for suspending the baskets. If you have a plaster ceiling, use an electric drill and rawl plugs to make the holes. Screw a hook into each hole.

2 Make sure each screw is firmly and securely in place, as the planted baskets will be heavy when they are watered. Suspend the baskets from the hooks.

AFTERCARE

Wait until the potting mix is nearly dry before watering the baskets again and water more regularly in warm weather. Feed the plants with a general-purpose indoor plant food every couple of weeks during spring and summer, following the manufacturer's instructions.

3 Put a saucer or dish with a raised lip around the edge in the bottom of each basket. This will collect water and prevent the basket getting wet.

4 Place a plant, still in its plastic pot, in each basket, using more plants in larger baskets, as I have with the two ferns. Consider the plants' leaf shapes and habits to create an interesting display.

5 Add some indoor plant food to a small bottle of water and shake well to mix, following the manufacturer's instructions on the quantities to use.

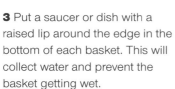

6 Water each plant until water starts to run out of the bottom of the plastic pot. Remember not to over-water the plants.

HEUCHERA stand

A lovely old washstand was the inspiration for this project and creates a stunning stand-alone display. The unusual peach-colored diascia were teamed with two heucherellas, the leaves of which bring additional texture and shape to the display. The planting has a beautiful, washed-out, sepia tone, but the pretty begonia adds a splash of bright pink.

1 Soak the rootballs of all the plants in water for about 10 minutes, or until they are wet through. Use the hammer and nail to make drainage holes in the bottom of the bowl (see page 8). Cover the holes with drainage crocks to prevent them getting blocked with potting mix.

2 Half-fill the bowl with potting mix and level off the surface.

YOU WILL NEED

Enamel bowl and a stand (such as an old washstand)

Hammer and heavy-duty nail

Drainage crocks

Potting mix

plants:

1 bright pink *Begonia* Pendula Group (tuberous begonia)

3 *Diascia* Aurora Series 'Aurora Apricot' (twinspur)

1 each of ✕ *Heucherella* 'Brass Lantern' and ✕ *H.* 'Honey Rose'

3 Take the diascias from their plastic pots and plant them on one side of the bowl.

4 Plant the begonia in the same way, this time at the front of the bowl, allowing the stems to trail over the edge.

5 Finally, remove the two heucherellas from their plastic pots and plant them on either side of the begonia, pushing the rootballs down so all the plants are sitting at the same level.

6 Add handfuls of potting mix to fill any gaps between the plants and press the surface down firmly. Water the bowl and let drain.

container WATER GARDEN

Having a pond in your garden widens the variety of beautiful plants you can enjoy and also attracts a lot more wildlife, such as pond skaters and damselflies, to your outside space. Don't let having a very small garden, balcony, or terrace prevent you from creating a decorative water feature—simply make a miniature water garden in a large tub. If you're using a wooden half-barrel, make sure it is completely waterproof; if not, you can treat the inside with a sealant such as tar or yacht varnish.

YOU WILL NEED

Large waterproof container, such as a galvanized metal tub or wooden half-barrel

Bricks

Rainwater (collected in a water butt) or tap water (that has been left to stand for a few days)

plants:

Eichhornia crassipes (water hyacinth)

Juncus ensifolius (sword-leaved rush)

Lobelia cardinalis 'Queen Victoria' (cardinal flower)

Lobelia × *speciosa* 'Vedrariensis'

Mentha cervina (Hart's pennyroyal)

Mimulus cardinalis (monkey flower)

Myriophyllum crispatum (upright water milfoil)

Pistia stratiotes (water lettuce)

1 Position the container in its final spot, which should be shady, before starting, as it will be too heavy to move when filled with water. If you are using tap water, rather than rainwater, fill the container with water first and leave it for a few days, so the chlorine levels can reduce through evaporation, before following the rest of the steps.

2 Put a few bricks in the bottom of the container. The aim is for the tops of the plant pots to sit a couple of inches below the surface of the water, so check the height of the bricks and arrange them accordingly. It can be helpful to put the plants in the container temporarily so you can check that the bricks are at the right level.

3 Take the tallest plant, still in its plastic pot, and place it at the back of the container.

4 Continue to place the plants in the container, moving them around until you are happy with the display.

5 When arranging the plants, try to put the taller plants toward the back and the shorter ones at the front. Do not put in the water lettuce and water hyacinth unless the container has already been filled with water (i.e. if you have used de-chlorinated tap water).

6 If you are using rainwater (rather than tap water) to fill the container, collect this from the water butt with a garden hose or using a watering can, and use it to fill the container.

7 Lastly, place the water lettuce and water hyacinth—still in their plastic pots, as for the other plants—in the container, ensuring their roots are fully submerged.

AFTERCARE

If the plants become too big, take them out of their plastic pots and divide them, re-potting them and putting only one back in the container. In very dry weather you may need to top up the container with more water. Use rainwater whenever possible, although a little tap water will not harm your water garden.

metal planter with
THISTLES and GRASSES

Thistles and grasses create a pretty planting scheme when teamed with fennel and grouped together in a large planter. This is a low-maintenance planting scheme that will look good throughout the summer and can be left in place the whole year round—just cut it back in early spring to allow for fresh growth.

YOU WILL NEED

Large galvanized metal planter

Hammer and heavy-duty nail (optional)

Drainage crocks

Potting mix

plants:

1 *Cirsium japonicum* 'Pink Beauty' (Japanese thistle)

2 *Eryngium × zabelii* 'Jos Eijking' (sea holly)

1 *Foeniculum vulgare* 'Purpureum' (bronze fennel)

3–4 *Lysimachia nummularia* 'Aurea' (golden creeping Jenny)

1 *Stipa tenuissima* (Mexican feather grass)

1 *Trifolium ochroleucum* (sulfur clover)

1 *Trifolium rubens* (clover)

1 Soak the rootballs of all the plants in water for about 20 minutes, or until they are wet through. If necessary, use the hammer and nail to make drainage holes in the bottom of the planter (see page 8). Cover the holes with drainage crocks to stop them becoming blocked with potting mix.

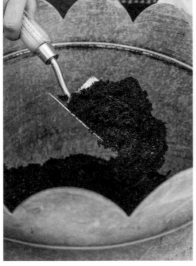

2 Fill the planter about two-thirds full with potting mix and level off the surface.

3 Take the eryngiums from their plastic pots and plant them on opposite sides of the planter toward the back, adding or removing potting mix, as required, so the tops of the plants' rootballs are sitting under the rim by an inch or two.

4 Plant the thistle in the same way, positioning it toward the back of the planter.

5 Take the Mexican feather grass from its plastic pot and plant it in the middle of the planter.

6 Plant the two clovers next, removing them from their plastic pots and positioning them at the front edge of the planter.

7 Remove the bronze fennel from its plastic pot and tuck it between the other plants. Here, I've planted it in front of one of the eryngiums. Gently loosen the roots if the plant is looking pot-bound.

8 Lastly, plant the creeping Jenny at the front of the planter, allowing the stems to trail over and soften the edge. Add a few handfuls of potting mix to fill any gaps between the plants and press the surface down firmly. Position the planter in a sunny spot, water, and let drain.

AFTERCARE

This planting display is fairly easy to look after. Simply check the potting mix in the planter regularly and water if it feels dry.

CHAPTER 3

SPECIAL OCCASION DISPLAYS

TIERED hanging basket

I was lucky enough to find a three-tiered hanging basket, which creates a stunning display when planted. If you cannot find one like this, you can create a similar effect by using chains to join together baskets of descending sizes. Choosing trailing plants with smallish rootballs means that you can fit lots of plants in each tier to produce a lovely, full hanging display.

YOU WILL NEED

Three-tiered wire hanging basket, with chains and hooks for suspending

Sheet moss (available from florists and garden centers)

Potting mix

Moisture-retaining granules (optional)

plants:

A selection of annuals in shades of pink and orange, such as *Calibrachoa* Can Can Series Double Apricot, *C.* Can Can Series Double Magenta, *C.* 'Orange', *C.* 'Raspberry Dawn', *C.* Superbells Series Apricot Punch, and *C.* Superbells Series Cherry Red (mini petunia), and pink geraniums

3 *Thymus pulegioides* 'Aureus' (golden large thyme)

1 Soak the rootballs of all the plants in water for about 10 minutes, or until they are wet through. Line the top basket with sheet moss, tearing off small pieces to fill in any gaps.

2 Add a couple of scoops of potting mix until the basket is nearly full.

3 Mix some moisture-retaining granules into the potting mix, following the manufacturer's instructions. This is not essential, but will help prevent the baskets, especially the smallest one, from drying out in hot weather.

4 Take the first plant from its plastic pot—here, I used a pink geranium, but an orange or pink mini petunia would work just as well—and make a small hole in the potting mix. Push the rootball into the hole and firm down the potting mix. You will probably need two plants for the top basket.

5 Plant the middle and bottom baskets in the same way, mixing up the orange and pink shades of the flowers to create a pleasing arrangement.

6 Plant a few golden thyme plants in the lower tiers to add another attractive shade of green to the display. Suspend the hanging basket, ensuring the hooks are strong enough to support the heavier weight of the three tiers when they are watered. Water all the tiers of the basket.

AFTERCARE

Keep the potting mix moist at all times—the smaller tiers, in particular, will be prone to drying out in hot weather. Use a general-purpose fertilizer every couple of weeks throughout the spring and summer to keep the plants healthy and flowering.

glass vase with FLOWERS

For a slightly different take on a terrarium, try planting flowering aquilegia and anemones, or other small-scale plants, in a wide-necked glass vase, letting the flowers bloom abundantly out of the top. Cover the bare potting mix with moss for a pretty indoor display that would also make a beautiful centerpiece for an al fresco lunch or dinner.

YOU WILL NEED

Large glass vase, with an open neck

Potting mix

Sheet moss (available from garden centers and florists)

plants:

Aethionema 'Warley Rose' (stone cress)

Anemone magellanica (windflower)

Aquilegia Swan Series 'Swan Violet and White' (columbine)

1 Soak the rootballs of the plants in water for about 10 minutes, or until they are wet through. Meanwhile, wash and dry the vase thoroughly. Put a few handfuls of potting mix in the bottom of the vase and spread it out evenly.

2 Remove the aquilegia from its plastic pot. Squeeze excess water from the rootball and carefully remove some of the potting mix to reduce its size. Put the aquilegia in the vase and press down the potting mix so the plant stays upright and in position.

3 Take the anemone out of its plastic pot and, again, squeeze out the excess water. Also remove some of the potting mix to reduce the size of the rootball. Plant the anemone in the vase, as before. Repeat for the stone cress.

4 Gently firm down the potting mix and cover the surface with pieces of moss. Press the moss down so that no potting mix is visible.

AFTERCARE

Check the potting mix every few days in warm weather and water sparingly when necessary.

POPPY and PETUNIA stone trough

Much as I love mixing colors when designing a planting scheme for a container, sometimes restricting the planting to one color and using just two different types of plant can work equally well. Although maintaining the moisture levels of the trough will keep the poppies in flower, these plants are just as beautiful once their petals have fallen off.

YOU WILL NEED

Stone or concrete trough
Drainage crocks
Potting mix

plants:

3 *Papaver nudicaule* 'Spring Fever Red' (Arctic poppy)
6 *Petunia* Surfinia Series Red

AFTERCARE

Keep the potting mix moist at all times and deadhead the petunias regularly. Once the poppies have gone over, their decorative seedheads will still be of interest. If you wish, replace them with more petunias or with other annuals with red flowers, such as zinnias or gazanias.

1 Soak the rootballs of all the plants in water for about 10 minutes, or until they are wet through. Cover the holes in the base of the trough with drainage crocks to prevent them becoming blocked with potting mix.

2 Add a few scoops of potting mix to the bottom of the trough, spreading it out evenly. Add more potting mix in stages, leveling it off each time, until the trough is about half full.

3 Take the poppies from their plastic pots and plant one at each end of the trough and one in the middle. Make sure the top of each rootball is sitting just under the rim of the trough.

4 Take a couple of petunias from their plastic pots and plant them between the poppies, pressing down the potting mix firmly so the plants fit snugly in the trough.

5 Continue to plant more petunias, letting them trail slightly over the edge of the trough.

6 Fill any gaps between the plants with more potting mix, firm in, and level off the surface. Water the trough and let drain.

PINK metal box

A battered metal box makes the perfect planter for this gorgeous selection of flowers, creating a beautiful, tiny summer garden that is perfect for bringing the outside in. The core of the planting is made up of rock roses (*Helianthemum*), which are available in a variety of wonderful shades and provide a real splash of color. The daisy-like flowers of the brachyscome and *Erigeron karvinskianus* add further interest to the display.

YOU WILL NEED

Small metal box

Collecting tray to fit base of box (if adding drainage holes and keeping the display indoors)

Hammer and heavy-duty nail (optional)

Drainage crocks (optional)

Potting mix

Moisture-retaining granules (optional)

plants:

Brachyscome 'Magenta Delight'

Erigeron karvinskianus (Mexican fleabane)

Helianthemum 'Hartswood Ruby', *H.* 'Highdown Apricot', *H.* 'Lawrenson's Pink', *H.* 'Salmon Queen', *H.* 'Sulphur Moon', and *H.* 'The Bride' (rock rose)

1 Soak the rootballs of all the plants in water for about 10 minutes, or until they are thoroughly wet. If you wish, use the hammer and nail to make drainage holes in the base of the box (see page 8). You do not have to make holes in the box, but it will improve drainage. If necessary, cover the holes with a few drainage crocks.

2 Half-fill the box with potting mix, adding moisture-retaining granules if you wish so that it does not dry out too quickly.

3 Take one of the helianthemums from its plastic pot and plant it in a corner of the box.

4 Continue planting the remaining helianthemums in the same way, arranging them pleasingly around the box.

5 Remove the brachyscome from its plastic pot and plant it at the front of the box. Finally, plant the erigeron, squeezing it in between the other plants.

AFTERCARE

Keep the potting mix moist and deadhead the flowers regularly to keep the plants in full bloom throughout the summer. If your box does not have drainage holes, make sure you do not over-water the display, because these plants do not like sitting in very wet soil.

6 Add a little more potting mix to fill any gaps and level the surface. Water the potting mix until it is just damp and do not let it dry out.

THYME wreath

This wreath is deceptively easy to make and creates a pretty focal point for a party or summer gathering. Either hang it on a door or gate to welcome guests or, alternatively, lay it flat on a table and put candles in the middle to create a charming centerpiece. (Never leave lit candles unattended.) To make a wreath to supply fresh thyme for cooking, omit the lobularia (so you don't end up eating that as well) and use more thyme plants. Ensure you buy enough plants to cover the wreath—here I used eight thyme plants and eight lobularias.

YOU WILL NEED

Sheet moss (available from florists and garden centers)

Wire wreath base, 16in (40cm) in diameter (available from good craft stores and online)

Potting mix

Fine copper wire

Galvanized wire, 1/16in (1mm) in diameter, and a hook or sturdy nail, for hanging the wreath (optional)

plants:

Lobularia maritima Easter Bonnet Series (sweet alyssum)

Thymus 'Bressingham', *T.* Coccineus Group, and *T.* 'Hartington Silver' (thyme)

Thymus serpyllum var. *albus* (white-flowered creeping thyme)

1 Soak the rootballs of all the plants in water for 10 minutes or so. Lay pieces of moss on a table in a circular shape, with the green mossy side facing down. Place the wreath base on top of the moss circle and add more moss, so you will have enough to cover both sides of the base.

2 Water the potting mix and let it drain so it is moist, but not soaking wet. Put handfuls of moist potting mix on top of the wreath, working your way all the way around.

3 Push the end of the roll of copper wire under the wreath and twist it around itself a few times to keep it firmly in place.

4 Wrap lengths of copper wire around the wreath, folding the moss over as you do so, to cover the base completely. Keep wrapping until the whole wreath is bound with moss.

5 Take a plant from its plastic pot and make it smaller by scraping off some of the potting mix from the rootball. Using your fingers, make a small hole in the moss on the wreath and push the roots of the plant inside. Thyme is pretty tough, so don't worry too much about damaging the roots, but try to keep them intact if you can. Continue to plant more thyme and lobularia plants around the wreath in the same way until the whole wreath is covered. As the plants grow, they will fill in any gaps.

6 Water the wreath while it is still lying flat and do not allow it to dry out. Suspend the wreath using a loop of galvanized wire over a hook or nail.

SMALL TREE containers

This is a great way to brighten up sparse branches on a small tree or to perk up a dull wall or corner of your garden. Plant small pails (buckets) with flowering plants, keeping to pinks, dark reds, and purples for a subtle look, or use bright, clashing oranges, reds, and yellows for a dazzling display.

YOU WILL NEED

Selection of small pails (buckets), with handles for suspending

Hammer and heavy-duty nail

Drainage crocks

Potting mix

Moisture-retaining granules (optional)

plants:

Calibrachoa MiniFamous Series Double Lemon and *C.* MiniFamous Series Double Pink Vein (mini petunia)

Pelargonium × *domesticum* 'Elegance Purple Majesty' (regal pelargonium)

Pelargonium Supreme Burgundy (ivy-leaved geranium)

Petunia Crazytunia Series Black Mamba and *P.* Supertunia Series Picasso in Blue

1 Soak the rootballs of all the plants in water for about 10 minutes, or until they are wet through. Use the hammer and nail to make drainage holes in the bottom of the pails (buckets)— for advice on how to do this, see page 8. Cover the base of each pail with drainage crocks to prevent the holes becoming blocked with potting mix.

2 Half-fill each pail with potting mix and press down gently to ensure there are no air pockets in the mix.

AFTERCARE

Keep the potting mix moist and use a general-purpose fertilizer every few weeks throughout the summer. Deadhead the plants regularly.

3 Add some moisture-retaining granules, if you wish, following the manufacturer's instructions on the packet. This will help keep the potting mix moist between waterings. This is especially useful for small containers such as these, which are liable to dry out quickly in warm weather.

4 Take the first plant from its plastic pot and place it in one of the pails. Add or take away potting mix, as required, so the top of the plant's rootball is sitting just below the rim of the pail.

5 Fill in around the plant with more potting mix and press down the surface gently. Plant the remaining pails in the same way. Place the planted pails in your chosen spot, either suspending them from a tree or perhaps lining them up on shelves against a house wall. Water the pails and let drain.

PLANTED ladder pots

To hide an unsightly area of the garden or a bare wall outside your home, it's fun to attach pots to a ladder and fill them with pretty flowering plants. The display will act as a planting screen and create a charming focal point. As these pots are small, they will need watering regularly—every day in warm weather—but they should stay in flower throughout the season.

YOU WILL NEED

Selection of small terracotta pots, with a lip or large rim

Galvanized metal wire, $\frac{1}{16}$in (1mm) in diameter

Wire cutters

Ladder

Potting mix

plants:

Bacopa Scopia Series Golden Leaves White

Calibrachoa MiniFamous Series Double Pink Vein (mini petunia)

Helichrysum petiolare 'Goring Silver' (everlasting flower)

Nicotiana × *sanderae* Cuba Series 'Cuba Deep Lime' (tobacco plant)

Petunia Potunia Series Piccola Purple Ice and *P.* Potunia Series Plus Yellow (mounding petunia)

Torenia Moon Series Rose Moon (wishbone flower)

1 Soak the rootballs of all the plants in water for about 10 minutes, or until they are thoroughly wet. Cut a length of wire, about 20in (50cm) long, and wrap it around one of the terracotta pots.

2 Twist the wire around itself so that it is held firmly in place around the pot.

3 Fasten the wire around a rung of the ladder, twisting it securely to hold the pot in place. If necessary, trim the ends of the wire. Attach the other pots to the rungs of the ladder in the same way, spacing them out evenly and creating a pleasing arrangement.

4 Take the first plant from its plastic pot and place it in one of the suspended pots. Push the plant down well into its new pot. Add a little potting mix to the bottom of the pot, if required.

AFTERCARE

Keep the potting mix moist at all times and deadhead the flowers regularly to guarantee further flushes of flowers through the season.

5 Continue planting the rest of the terracotta pots in the same way until the display is finished. Water the pots well and let drain.

GERANIUMS and PETUNIAS in pots

Sometimes the simplest ideas are the best. Grouping plants with similar beautifully rich colors can create a stunning display and is a great way to brighten up steps or ledges in a garden or outside space.

YOU WILL NEED

Selection of terracotta and clay pots

Drainage crocks

Potting mix

plants:

Pelargonium Aristo Series Aristo Shoko, *P.* × *domesticum* 'Elegance Purple Majesty', and *P.* 'Regalia Dark Red' (regal pelargonium)

Pelargonium Supreme Burgundy (ivy-leaved pelargonium)

Petunia Crazytunia Series Black Mamba and *P.* Sweetunia Series Johnny Flame

1 Soak the rootballs of all the plants in water for about 10 minutes, or until they are thoroughly wet. Put a drainage crock in the bottom of each pot to prevent potting mix clogging up the hole. If any of your pots do not have a drainage hole, omit this step and be careful not to over-water.

2 Put a scoop of potting mix in the bottom of each pot and level off the surface.

3 Remove the first plant from its plastic pot—in this case, one of the ivy-leaved pelargoniums—and put it in one of the terracotta pots.

4 Carefully fill any gaps around the plant's rootball with a few handfuls of potting mix and firm down the surface. Plant several pots in the same way to create a striking and colorful display. Water all the pots and let drain. Remember to water pots without drainage holes only sparingly.

AFTERCARE

Deadheading the flowers regularly through the flowering season will ensure a repeating display of colorful flowers.

CHAPTER 4

FRUITS AND HARVESTS

AFTERCARE

Check the potting mix in the containers regularly and keep it moist, but not too wet. Every few weeks, use a general-purpose fertilizer to promote lots of bushy growth in the herbs.

herbs in CONCRETE POTS

The simple shapes and neutral colors of these concrete pots let the soft hues of the herbs shine out. Choose herbs you enjoy eating and plant them with plenty of gravel in the bottom of the pots to allow for drainage, as they will not like sitting in very wet potting mix.

YOU WILL NEED

Concrete pots in a range of different sizes

Drainage crocks

Gravel

Potting mix

plants:

Back pot: *Thymus citriodorus* 'Variegatus' (variegated lemon thyme), *T.* 'Silver Queen' (thyme), and *T. vulgaris* (common thyme)

Front pot: *Salvia officinalis* (common sage)

Left pot: *Lavandula angustifolia* (English lavender)

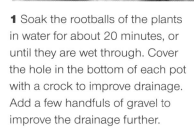

1 Soak the rootballs of the plants in water for about 20 minutes, or until they are wet through. Cover the hole in the bottom of each pot with a crock to improve drainage. Add a few handfuls of gravel to improve the drainage further.

2 Half-fill the pots with potting mix and level off the surface.

3 Remove the first herbs from their plastic pots and plant them in one of the pots. Fill around the rootballs with more potting mix, firming it down and leveling off the surface.

4 Cover the potting mix with a decorative layer of gravel to help retain moisture. Plant the remaining herbs in the other pots. Water the pots and let drain.

hanging basket with CHERRY TOMATOES

This is a great summer container if you are short of outdoor space. Suspend the basket using a metal wall bracket or hook by your door for a handy supply of tomatoes throughout the summer. Alternatively, make a tripod like the one shown here, firmly securing the ends of the branches in the ground, as the basket will become quite heavy, especially when it is watered.

YOU WILL NEED

Hanging basket and liner

Potting mix

Moisture-retaining granules (optional)

Metal wall bracket or hook, for suspending the basket (optional)

3 sturdy branches and garden twine, to make a supporting tripod (optional)

Metal butcher's hook, for suspending the basket from the tripod (optional)

plants:

6 *Solanum lycopersicum* (tomato plant), such as 'Losetto', 'Tumbling Tiger', and 'Tumbling Tom Red'

Tropaeolum majus (nasturtium) seeds (optional)

1 Soak the rootballs of all the tomato plants in water for about 10 minutes, or until they are wet through. Place the liner in the hanging basket and press it firmly into place.

2 Fill the basket with potting mix. If you wish, add some moisture-retaining granules, following the manufacturer's instructions. Level off the surface.

3 Remove a tomato plant from its plastic pot, scoop out a little of the potting mix from the basket, and plant the tomato in the hole. Make sure the top of the plant's rootball is level with the surface of the potting mix.

4 Continue to plant the remaining tomatoes in the basket, using five or six plants in one hanging basket. If necessary, fill any gaps between the plants with a little more potting mix and firm in.

5 If you wish, plant three nasturtium seeds in the basket; they will add further color to the display when they flower.

6 Hang the basket in a warm, sunny spot, either against a wall, using a metal bracket or hook, or from a simple tripod, as I have here. To make one, tie three sturdy branches together securely with garden twine, then suspend the basket from the tripod by hooking a butcher's hook over the twine and branches. Water the basket and let drain.

AFTERCARE

Keep the potting mix in the hanging basket moist, but not too wet. When flowers begin appearing on the tomato plants, start feeding them weekly with a tomato fertilizer to encourage fruiting.

STRAWBERRY tower

To maximize the growing potential of a small space, stack some galvanized metal tubs in different sizes on top of one another and fill them with strawberry plants to create a tower of summer fruits. Use a few different varieties of strawberry so they will ripen at different times and provide you with a steady supply of fruit.

YOU WILL NEED

3 galvanized metal tubs, in descending sizes

Hammer and heavy-duty nail (optional)

Drainage crocks

Potting mix

plants:

A selection of approximately 10 strawberry plants, such as:

Fragaria × *ananassa* Delizz, *F.* × *ananassa* Fragoo Deep Rose, *F.* × *ananassa* Fragoo White, and *F.* × *ananassa* 'Toscana' (garden strawberry)

Fragaria vesca (alpine strawberry)

1 Soak the rootballs of all the strawberry plants in water for about 10 minutes, or until they are wet through. If necessary, use the hammer and nail to make drainage holes in the bottom of the tubs (see page 8). Add a few drainage crocks to the bottom of the tubs. Fill the largest tub with potting mix and use the palm of your hand to flatten it down firmly in the middle. Fill the other two tubs with potting mix.

2 Take the medium-sized tub and place it on top of the largest one. Make sure the base of the tub is held securely in place so that it will not topple over.

3 Flatten down the middle of the potting mix in the medium-sized tub, as before, and place the smallest tub on top.

4 Again, push the smallest tub down well to ensure that it is held firmly in place.

5 Scoop out a little potting mix from the largest tub. Remove the first strawberry plant from its plastic pot and insert it in the hole. Firm the potting mix around the plant with your fingers.

6 Continue to add strawberry plants around the edges of the tubs, using about five plants in the largest tub and three plants in the middle tub. Plant one strawberry plant in the small top tub, allowing it to trail over the sides. Water the three tubs.

AFTERCARE

Keep the potting mix in the tubs moist. Feed the strawberry plants with a high-potash fertilizer once the flowers develop, and position the tower in a sunny spot to encourage the fruit to ripen.

raised bed for EDIBLES

I would love a garden that's big enough for a large vegetable patch, but this raised bed provides enough space to grow a surprising amount of delicious produce. Plants in a raised bed can be grown closer together than if you were growing them in open ground. This allows you to cram in lots of plants and provides a steady supply of vegetables in summer. You can either grow the young vegetable plants from seed before transferring them to the bed or, alternatively, buy garden-ready plug plants from a garden center or nursery, or online.

YOU WILL NEED

Seed trays (optional)

Seed potting mix (optional)

Watering can, with fine rose attachment (optional)

Plant labels and waterproof pen (optional)

Clear plastic bags or plastic wrap/clingfilm (optional)

Raised bed

Garden soil or good-quality topsoil (optional)

Plastic pots and potting mix, for potting on (optional)

Garden compost or well-rotted manure

Stout branches and garden twine, to support the beans

plants:

A selection of vegetable seeds or young plug plants, such as:

Brassica oleracea Acephala Group (kale), such as 'Red Russian'

Brassica oleracea Capitata Group (cabbage), such as 'Advantage'

Cucurbita maxima 'Uchiki Kuri' (onion squash)

Lactuca sativa (lettuce), such as 'Little Gem', 'Lollo Rossa', and 'Red Salad Bowl'

Phaseolus coccineus (runner bean), such as 'White Emergo'

Tropaeolum majus (nasturtium)

1 If you have bought your vegetables as young plug plants, skip Steps 1 and 2, and begin with Step 3. If you are growing some or all of your crops from seed, follow the instructions on the packet for the best time to sow each type. To sow the seed, fill a seed tray with seed potting mix and firm it down gently. Pour some seed into the palm of your hand—in this case, lettuce—and sprinkle it sparingly over the potting mix, roughing up the surface slightly to cover the seed. Water the seed tray, using a watering can with a fine rose attachment to avoid disturbing the seed. Insert a plant label with the name of the seed and the date of sowing in the tray. Cover each seed tray with a clear plastic bag or piece of plastic wrap (clingfilm). Leave the tray(s) somewhere warm for the seeds to germinate, removing the cover from each tray as soon as the seedlings emerge.

2 When the seedlings are a couple of inches tall, either pot them on into individual plastic pots using fresh potting mix and keep them under cover, if it is still cold outside, or plant them directly in the raised bed.

3 To prepare the raised bed for planting, simply remove any weeds if it already contains soil or, if you are starting the bed from scratch, fill it with garden soil or topsoil. Of the vegetables in this selection, lettuce does not need a particularly rich soil, so decide where you're going to plant the lettuce—here, I've planted it toward the front of the bed—and dig lots of garden compost or well-rotted manure into the soil in the rest of the bed.

4 Plant the lettuce seedlings or plug plants in rows in your chosen position. Space the plants about 6–8in (15–20cm) apart in each row, but check the instructions on the packet or label for planting distances for specific varieties. As you're planting in a raised bed, rather than in open ground, you'll easily be able to reach the plants and so don't need to have set distances between the rows.

5 To plant the runner beans, insert supporting branches in the soil along one side of the bed, so the plants will be able to grow up them. Make sure the branches are standing up straight.

6 Dig a small hole near one of the branches and pop in a bean plant. Firm in the soil around the plant's stem. Plant two runner bean plants next to each branch. As the runner beans grow upward, tie them to their supports with garden twine.

7 Plant the young cabbage, kale, and squash plants in neat rows next to the lettuce and runner beans, following the advice on planting distances given in Step 4, and firm them in well. Include a few nasturtium plants to add a splash of color to the bed. These are also edible, bringing a peppery taste to summer salads. Water the whole bed.

AFTERCARE

In warm weather, water the raised bed daily. Keep your eye out for pest damage and remove snails, slugs, and caterpillars if you spot them. Harvest the lettuces when they are ready, but before they get too big. If you have used cut-and-come-again lettuce varieties, harvest them regularly for a good supply of salad leaves through the summer.

POTTED KUMQUAT

For a touch of the Mediterranean, how about growing a citrus tree? Kumquat trees grow happily in pots and will reward you with lots of fruit if a high-nitrogen fertilizer is used regularly throughout spring and summer. They can be kept outside in a sunny, sheltered spot during the warmer months, but will appreciate being moved indoors over winter. I underplanted the kumquat shown here with daisy-like bidens and erigeron, and trailing ivy.

1 Soak the rootballs of all the plants in water for about 10 to 20 minutes, or until they are wet through. The kumquat will need at least 20 minutes. Cover the holes in the bottom of the pot with a few drainage crocks to prevent them becoming blocked with potting mix.

2 Fill the pot approximately half full with potting mix, incorporating some grit, sand, or gravel (whatever you have at hand) as you do so to improve drainage.

YOU WILL NEED

Terracotta pot

Drainage crocks

Potting mix

Grit, coarse sand, or gravel

Pebbles

plants:

3 *Bidens* 'Moonlight' (tickseed)

1 *Citrus japonica* (kumquat tree)

3 *Erigeron karvinskianus* (Mexican fleabane)

6–8 *Hedera* (ivy)

3 Take the kumquat from its plastic pot, gently breaking up the rootball first, and plant it in the middle of the terracotta pot.

4 Remove the erigeron and bidens from their plastic pots next and plant them around the edge of the pot, allowing the stems to trail over the edge slightly.

5 Plant the ivies around the edge of the pot in the same way, tucking them between the other plants. Add more potting mix to fill any gaps between the plants, as required. Firm in the plants and level the surface of the potting mix.

6 Cover the surface of the potting mix with some pretty pebbles, which not only adds a decorative touch, but also helps to keep the potting mix moist.

AFTERCARE

Water the pot generously over the summer and feed regularly with a high-nitrogen fertilizer. Over the winter, let the surface of the potting mix dry out between waterings.

NASTURTIUM cone

Nasturtiums are very easy to grow and go on flowering right through the summer months. They are strikingly pretty, with the added advantage that the flowers are edible and can transform a plain salad into something very special. Nasturtiums do not need very rich soil, and will flower better in poorer soil, so it is fine to use potting mix that has been used for previous container displays. I have made planting suggestions for a cone-shaped hanging basket with a diameter of 11in (28cm).

YOU WILL NEED

Metal, cone-shaped hanging basket, with chains and hooks for suspending

Pail (bucket), large enough to hold the hanging basket (optional)

A couple of small drainage crocks

Gravel

Potting mix

plants:

3 variegated *Hedera* (ivy)

3 *Lysimachia nummularia* 'Aurea' (golden creeping Jenny)

4 *Tropaeolum* Flame Thrower Series and/or *T. majus* (nasturtium)

1 Soak the rootballs of all the plants in water for about 10 minutes, or until they are wet through. If you wish, place the cone in a pail (bucket) to provide support. Otherwise, it can be helpful to ask someone to hold the cone while you work. Put the small drainage crocks over the hole at the bottom of the cone, so that it will not become blocked with potting mix.

2 Add a few handfuls of gravel to the bottom of the cone. This will stop the potting mix from becoming too compacted.

3 Put a few trowel-fuls of potting mix in the cone until it is nearly full.

4 Remove the nasturtiums from their plastic pots, use your fingers to make a hole in the potting mix near the edge of the cone, and plant the first nasturtium. Press the potting mix down firmly around the plant. Repeat with two more nasturtiums.

5 Plant the ivies in the same way, near the edge of the container, but trail them over the rim of the cone.

6 Plant the lysimachias in the gaps between the other plants, again allowing the stems to trail over the sides of the cone.

7 Plant one more nasturtium in the middle of the other plants and firm down the potting mix. Suspend the cone in a sunny or partially shaded spot using the chains and hooks. Water the hanging basket and let drain.

AFTERCARE

Keep the potting mix damp, watering daily in hot weather. All parts of the nasturtium plant are edible, with a peppery taste, so enjoy picking the brightly colored flowers to eat in summer salads or as decorative garnish. Regular picking will encourage more flowers!

PEPPER and BASIL metal planter

YOU WILL NEED

Shallow metal planter

Hammer and heavy-duty nail (optional)

Drainage crocks

Potting mix

Gravel

Short garden canes and raffia, for tying in the peppers (optional)

plants:

1 each of *Capsicum annuum* 'Cajun Belle', *C. annuum* 'Cheyenne', and *C. annuum* 'Loco' (chili pepper)

2 *Capsicum annuum* var. *annuum* (Grossum Group) 'Sweet Banana' (bell/sweet pepper)

1 *Capsicum chinense* 'Scotch Bonnet Red' (Scotch bonnet)

1 *Ocimum basilicum* (sweet basil)

Growing a selection of bell (sweet) peppers and chili peppers will give you a plentiful harvest throughout the summer. Planting a few basil plants with the peppers is supposed to improve the flavor of the chili peppers and may also help to deter troublesome aphids and spider mites.

1 Soak the rootballs of all the plants in water for about 10 minutes, or until they are wet through. If necessary, use the hammer and nail to make drainage holes in the bottom of the planter (see page 8). Cover the holes with crocks to improve drainage and stop them becoming blocked with potting mix.

2 Half-fill the planter with potting mix and spread it out evenly.

3 Remove one of the chili peppers from its plastic pot and plant it toward one side of the planter.

4 Continue to plant the remaining chili peppers in the planter.

5 Remove the bell (sweet) peppers from their plastic pots and plant them among the chili peppers.

6 Remove the basil from its pot and plant it in the container among the pepper plants.

AFTERCARE

Ensure the potting mix is kept moist and feed the plants weekly with a high-potassium fertilizer to encourage fruiting. Keep the display in a warm, sunny spot and move it inside in the colder months. As the pepper plants grow, you may find they need staking. To do this, use pieces of raffia to tie the plants to garden canes or twiggy branches pushed into the potting mix.

7

8

7 Fill any gaps between the plants with more potting mix, as required, pressing down the surface to hold the plants in place.

8 Spread gravel over the surface of the potting mix, pouring it carefully around the stalks of the plants. Water the container and let drain.

resources

UNITED KINGDOM
Alexandra Nurseries
Estate House
Parish Lane
Penge
London SE20 7LJ
020 8778 4145
www.alexandranurseries.co.uk
*Lovely selection of plants and
vintage gardening accessories*

Anthropologie
00 800 0026 8476
www.anthropologie.com
*Stylish garden accessories, pots,
and containers*

Columbia Road Flower Market
Columbia Road
London E2 7RG
www.columbiaroad.info
*Fantastic selection of plants at very
good prices*

Crocus
01344 578111
www.crocus.co.uk
*A wide selection of plants, seeds,
and garden accessories available
mail order*

Heucheraholics
Boldre Nurseries
Southampton Road
Lymington
Hampshire SO41 8ND
01590 670581
www.heucheraholics.co.uk
*Specialist nursery with a good range
of heucheras, heucherellas, and
tiarellas*

Mabel and Rose
01993 878861
www.mabelandrose.com
*Lovely selection of vintage
containers and gardening tools*

Mason and Painter
67 Columbia Road
London E2 7RG
www.masonandpainter.co.uk
*Beautiful range of vintage planters,
tubs, and cans (tins)*

Petersham Nurseries
Church Lane (off Petersham Road)
Richmond
Surrey TW10 7AB
020 8940 5230
www.petershamnurseries.com
*Lovely selection of plants with
garden accessories and containers*

RHS Wisley
Woking
Surrey GU23 6QB
0845 260 9000
www.rhs.org.uk/gardens/wisley
*Huge selection of plants and garden
accessories with a good advice
center*

Sarah Raven's Kitchen Garden
0345 092 0283
www.sarahraven.com
*Beautiful selection of seeds,
seedlings, and plants all available
mail order*

Sunbury Antiques Market
Kempton Park Racecourse
Staines Road East
Sunbury-on-Thames
Middlesex TW16 5AQ
01932 230946
www.sunburyantiques.com
*Huge second-hand market twice
a month with lots of vintage garden
containers, old cans (tins), and
garden accessories*

UNITED STATES AND CANADA
Anthropologie (across USA)
(800) 309-2500
www.anthropologie.com
*Beautiful selection of garden
accessories and pots*

Ben Wolff Pottery
279 Sharon Turnpike
Goshen
Connecticut 06756
(860) 618-2317
www.benwolffpottery.com
*Lovely handmade pots and
containers*

Flora Grubb Gardens
1634 Jerrold Avenue
San Francisco
California 94124
(415) 626-7256
www.floragrubb.com
*A good selection of planters
and containers*

GRDN
103 Hoyt Street
Brooklyn
New York 11217
(718) 797-3628
www.grdnbklyn.com
*A beautiful selection of garden
accessories*

Jayson Home
1885 N Clybourn Avenue
Chicago
Illinois 60614
(800) 472-1885
www.jaysonhome.com
*A wide range of reclaimed pots
and planters*

Potted
3158 Los Feliz Boulevard
Los Angeles
California 90039
(323) 665-3801
www.pottedstore.com
*Lovely selection of pots, containers,
and accessories*

Pottery Barn (across USA)
(888) 779-5176
www.potterybarn.com
*A great selection of garden
accessories*

Pure Modern (online/Canada)
(800) 563-0593
www.puremodern.com
*Pots, planters, and garden
accessories*

West Elm (across USA)
(888) 922-4119
www.westelm.com
*Garden pots and tubs, plus garden
accessories*

index

acknowledgments

I was so delighted to be asked to do a book on summer gardening. Thank you very much indeed to Cindy Richards at CICO Books—I am very grateful. Not only was it a chance to work with beautiful plants, but also an opportunity to work with the wonderful Debbie Patterson again, which is always a treat. I couldn't have asked for a more lovely editor than Caroline West, who is unstintingly patient, knowledgeable, and thorough, and offers support and advice in such a gentle way.

The beautiful page layouts and sensitive design are by Luana Gobbo, while the fabulous locations were efficiently coordinated by Kerry Lewis. The whole book was overseen by Anna Galkina, whose organization and support helped to make the whole process much easier. Thank you all so very much.

Thanks also go to the lovely Andrea Mason for providing laughs, lifts, and plant-buying opportunities, and also the beautiful metal plant stand. And thank you to the Hardy Dahl gang. For all the things.